How I Learned to Be Considerate of Others

by Lawrence E. Shapiro, Ph.D.

The Center for Applied Psychology, Inc.
King of Prussia, PA

How I Learned to Be Considerate of Others

By Lawrence E. Shapiro, Ph.D.
Storybook illustrations by Jille Mandel
Workbook illustrations by Greg V. Valentine
Designed by Christopher Laughlin

Published by:
The Center for Applied Psychology, Inc.
P.O. Box 61587, King of Prussia, PA 19406 U.S.A.
Tel. 1-800-962-1141

The Center for Applied Psychology, Inc. is the publisher of Childswork/Childsplay, a catalog of products for mental health professionals, teachers, and parents who wish to help children with their social and emotional growth.

ISBN: 1-882732-27-8

INTRODUCTION

HOW I LEARNED TO BE CONSIDERATE OF OTHERS is a storybook and a workbook in one. The first half of the book—the story book—tells the story of Janet, a little girl who is often selfish. Janet learns that when she thinks only of herself, she is very lonely, but that when she thinks of others, she is surrounded by people who love her.

The second half of the book—the activity section—teaches values. It addresses the importance of seeing another person's point of view, the reasons why thinking positively benefits you and those around you, and the value of doing good deeds.

HOW I LEARNED TO BE CONSIDERATE OF OTHERS was written by Lawrence E. Shapiro, Ph.D., a nationally known expert in child development and the author of more than two dozen books and therapeutic games for children.

Why can't I have things my way?

I want chocolate cupcakes for breakfast. I want a birthday every month, not every year. I want my little brother to stay in his room whenever I am around.

Why do I have to go to school if I don't feel like it?
School is stupid anyway.

I don't see why I have to do homework everyday! When am I
supposed to watch TV? Why can't I just do homework on
Wednesdays? For just half an hour.

And why does everybody have to bother me so much?

Why does my mother always say, "Do your chores, and I mean now!"? My chores are stupid and I hate them.

Why does my teacher always give me a mean look and say, "Don't pass notes, Janet" and "Keep your hands to yourself, Janet" and "Don't make such nasty faces, Janet."

Why doesn't she mind her own business?

And why did Melina get mad at me because I took her candy from her locker? She had plenty.

And why did my Dad yell at me because I spilled
something in his car? I didn't mean to do it!

WHY CAN'T EVERYONE JUST LEAVE ME ALONE?!

Well. . . I guess I don't really like being alone.

I guess I do want people to like me.

Lots of people like Melina. I'll watch her and do what she does!

And I'll ask my mom and dad what to do!

Then one day at school, we had a lesson on "being positive."
My teacher, Ms. Haverty, said that some people always see the
negative side and some people always see the positive side.
Most people like to be around people who are positive.

23

I try always to remember the "Five Ways to be Positive"
that Ms. Haverty taught us.

RULE #1: Look for the good in a situation.

RULE #2: Tell people when you like something they did.

RULE #3: Try not to be a complainer; try to be a problem-solver.

RULE #4: Do at least one kind act every day.

This sure is a hard way to spend a Saturday, writing a book report. But I'm going to do a really good job and get an "A." I'll work for two more hours and then I'll be done and have the rest of the weekend to have fun.

RULE #5: If you feel down or mad, say positive things to yourself to feel better.

A very funny thing happened, when I tried to be positive. . .

Can you guess what?

How i Learned to Be Considerate of Others

Activity Book

1. Ways To Help

My teacher says that helping other people is like having a bowl of ice cream that is always full no matter how much you eat. You can *always* find a way to help someone else, and it will just about *always* make you feel good.

There are many, many ways to help people. Can you think of 20 different ways? The pictures below will help you get started.

Twenty Ways To Help Other People

1. _____
2. _____
3. _____
4. _____
5. _____
6. _____
7. _____
8. _____
9. _____
10. _____
11. _____
12. _____
13. _____
14. _____
15. _____
16. _____
17. _____
18. _____
19. _____
20. _____

2. Keep on Smiling

My mom says that the best thing about me is my smile. She says that a smile is always your best friend, which means that a smile will always make you feel better. My mom says that there are a lot of songs and expressions about smiling. I wrote some of them below, but in each one, some of the letters are left out. Can you match each expression with the right picture? Do you know what the expressions mean? If you don't, ask an adult to explain them.

Let a smile be your u _ _ _ _ _ _ _.

Smile and the w _ _ _ _ smiles with you.

When you're smiling, the s _ _ comes shinning through.

I'd walk a million m _ _ _ _ for one of her smiles.

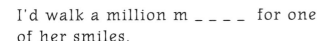

3. Caring For Others

When you see something that is wrong, or someone who needs help, it is easy to look away. But when you help other people, you feel better about yourself, no matter how bad your own problems may be.

Susie and Sally were having a discussion about different problems in the world. Everything that grumpy Susie had to say was negative. But everything Sally said was positive. Can you write in a positive statement for each negative thing that Susie had to say? The first one is filled in for you.

Susie:
I don't worry about homeless people. They have to take care of themselves.

Sally:
I helped with a food drive at school to give food to a shelter.

If people are poor, they should just work harder.

_____
_____
_____

Pollution doesn't bother me. I'll just move to another place.

_____
_____
_____

I don't care if cigarettes are bad for you. They won't hurt me.

_____
_____
_____

4. What Children Need

Did you know that of all the animals in the world, human babies need the most care! All other baby animals get food and protection from their parents, but they are born with everything else that they need. Here is a baby with nothing but his "birthday suit." Can you draw in all of the things that he needs to be safe and healthy? On the next page, draw in what *you* need to be happy and healthy.

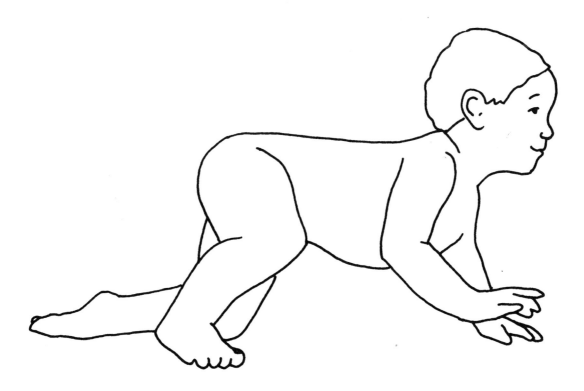

What You Need to Be Happy and Healthy

5. What Other People Need

Babies aren't the only people who need care. Everyone needs to be taken care of sometimes, children, parents, and grandparents, too. Can you identify all the things in this picture and explain how they are used to take care of or to help someone?

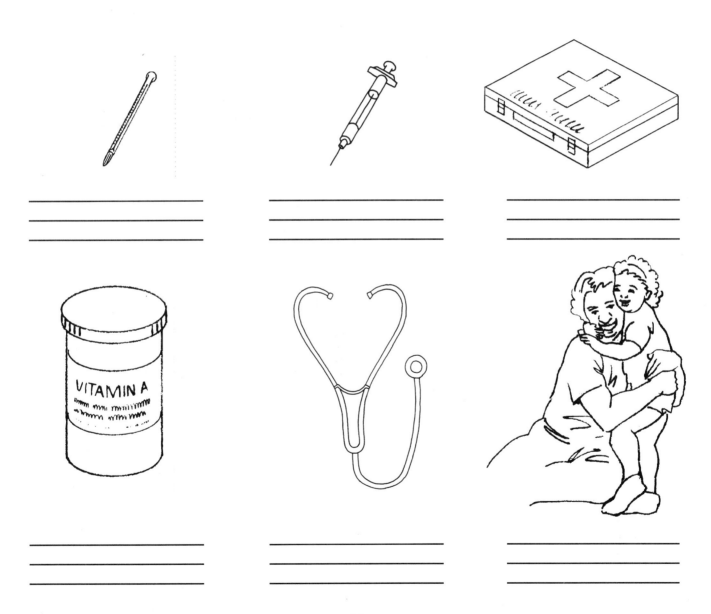

41

6. Listening to Others

Sometimes you may be so interested in what you are saying or doing, that you may not be paying attention to what someone else is saying or doing. These children were all interrupted before they got to finish what they were saying. But you can finish their sentences for them.

I'm sorry _____

I don't feel _____

Watch out _____

I'm sad _____

7. Listening to Others With Your Eyes

Another way you can listen to others is by watching. This sounds strange, but it is true. You can "hear" what people are trying to tell you, by watching their expression or how they move their bodies. This is called non-verbal language, because it is language without words. What are these three children saying by their "body language?"

8. Saying Things to Help Others Feel Better

Question: Do you know what is one of the nicest gifts that you can give someone and it doesn't cost a cent?

Answer: A kind word.

When you say something nice to someone it makes them feel good about themselves, good about you, and good about people in general. Here are some "gifts" to get you started. Fill in each sentence to make it a "gift" for someone else.

I really like your _____

Thank you for the _____

The thing I like about you best is _____

I admire you when _____

You're a great _____

I love you because you're _____

9. Waiting Your Turn

Do you know anyone who is really pushy and demanding? Have you ever had someone barge in line in front of you at the movies? No one likes people who can't wait their turn. They are really inconsiderate and only thinking of themselves.

Here is a picture of Impatient Ernestine. She always thinks that she should go first and she always has a reason why she thinks that she is right. Write down what you would say to each of her reasons:

I really have to go to the bathroom badly! I need to be first!

_____

_____

_____

_____

I want a good seat!

_____

_____

_____

I should bat first! I didn't get to go first for a whole week!

_____

_____

_____

I have to run home or I'll be late for dinner!

_____

_____

_____

10. Showing Respect

Julie was a girl who always treated other people with respect and everyone liked her for it. It seemed that Julie always knew exactly what to do at the right time. Julie started to draw a picture in each of the boxes below that demonstrates how she shows respect. Can you finish each picture for her?

Respect for
someone else's property.

Respect for authority

Respect for older people

Respect for
the environment

Respect for other
people's feelings

47

11. Sharing

Everyone likes kids who share. Allan started to draw the things he liked to share, but then his mom called him to dinner. Can you finish the things that he was drawing?

12. Kindness Every Day

Paul decided that he would be a better person by doing something kind for someone else every day. Here are the kind things that Paul did for five days in a row. Can you match each one to the right person or object?

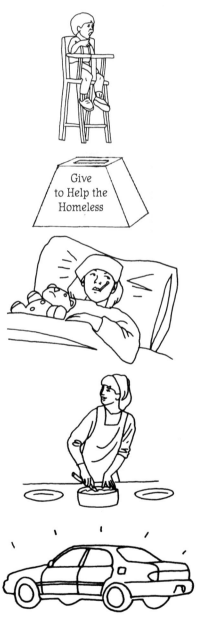

49

13. Taking Care of the Environment

Everyone knows that it is important to take good care of our planet. After all, we only have one! List 10 things that kids can do to be considerate of our world. The pictures will give you a hint.

_____

_____

_____

_____

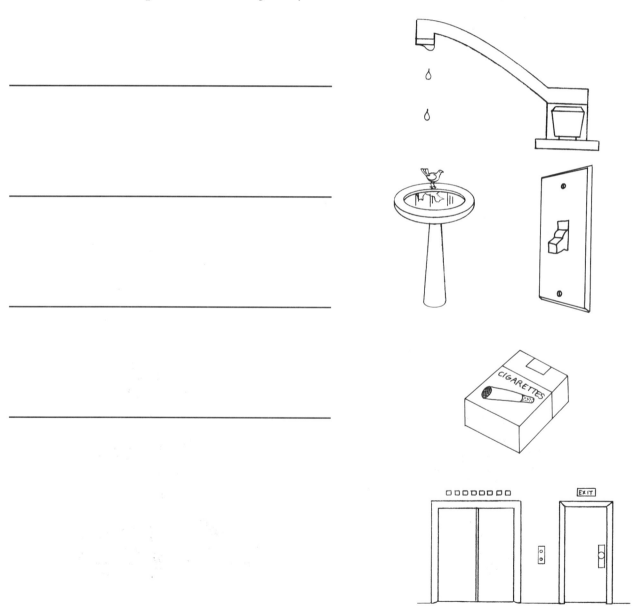

14. Good Manners

Having good manners is one of the most important ways that you can show people that you care about their feelings. Everyone likes children who are polite, have good table manners, and who show concern for others.

Did you know that Sir Walter Raleigh was knighted by the Queen of England because he placed his coat on a mud puddle so that she wouldn't get her feet wet!

Below are some ways that you can show other people that you have good manners. They are written in a puzzle form. Can you figure out each puzzle to help you remember these good manners? The answers are on the bottom of the page.

_____

_____ "O"   D+

_____ &   "U"

15. Showing Compassion

Sometimes there are others who really need our help. Some people see when help is needed and always offer a hand. Do you always offer to help out? What would you do in the following situation? Connect the dots to see who needs your help and to figure out what you can do.

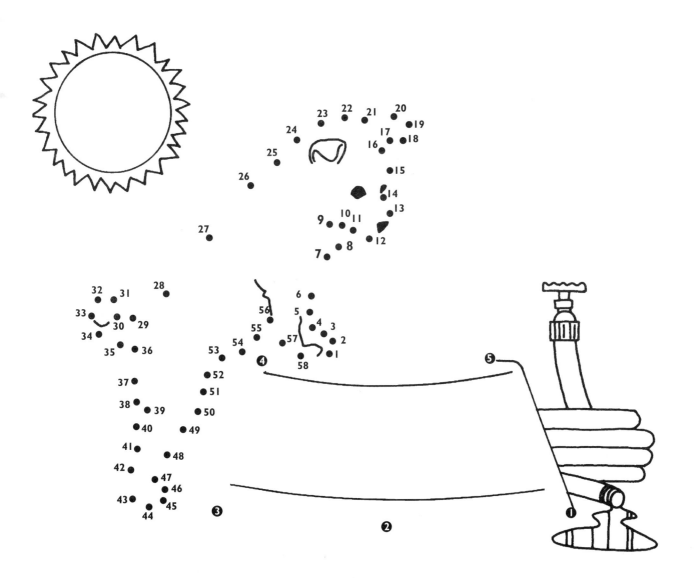

53

16. Saying You're Sorry

Everyone does something wrong sometimes. But when you make a mistake, you can say that you are sorry and then do something to make things better. These children all made a mistake. What can each of them do to make things better? Draw it in the box next to each child.

"You're late again!"

17. Getting Your Chores Done

Most children have chores that they do around the house, such as taking out the garbage, or setting the dinner table. When you do your chores the right way, and on time, you make life easier for everyone else in your family.
Use this chart to make a list of your chores and what days they have to be done. Then give yourself a happy face everytime that you do them. When you get all your chores done on time at the end of the week, show your chart to everyone in your family. I'll bet that they have Happy Faces too!

CHORES CHART	M	T	W	Th	F	S	Su
1							
2							
3							
4							
5							
6							
7							
8							
9							
10							

18. Extra Special Things That Make Others Smile

Have you ever had someone do something extra special for you? Maybe your mom put an extra dessert in your lunch? Or maybe your dad let you stay up past your bedtime to see a great movie?

Everyone likes it when something special happens, and they really like the person who makes it happen!

Here are a few "extra special" things that you can do for people. See if you can think of five more.

• Do someone else's chores.
• Helping somebody with their homework.
• Sharing your candy with a friend.

1. _____

2. _____

3. _____

4. _____

5. _____

19. Giving Gifts

Another way to show someone that you care is by giving them a gift. Perhaps it is a birthday gift or a gift for their anniversary. Or maybe it's a gift just to say, "I LIKE YOU."

There are many beautiful and useful gifts that you can make yourself. Here is one of my favorites that you can make in just a few minutes. It's called a Wind Chime. It looks nice and makes beautiful music when hung by a window or on a porch. Give it to a friend, your teacher, your grandma or grandpa, anyone you like and who likes you.

How to Make a Wind Chime:

You will need:
About a yard of rope
A lid to a coffee can
6 to 8 seashells, bottle caps,
  large screws, or silverware,
  or other things that will
  "clang" together
Scissors (use with adult supervision)
Glue

20. it's The Thought That Counts

Have you ever been to a card shop and seen all the thousands of cards that people buy for each other? There are birthday cards, "Get Well" cards, and "Thank You" cards, Christmas cards and Valentines Day cards. Cards are a great way to say, "I'm thinking about you."

On the following pages are 3 cards for you to complete and different pictures to cut out and make designs. Make a photocopy of each page and then make cards to share your important messages.

I'm Sorry!

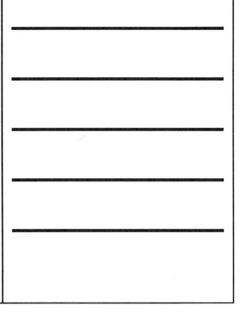

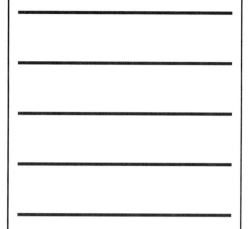

Happy Birthday!

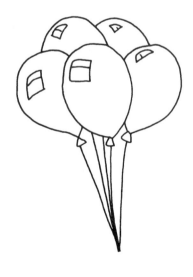

21. Taking Another Person's Point of View

Did you know that it is very common for two people to see the exact same thing differently? Usually when people fight, one person sees things one way and the other person sees it differently.

For example, Billy and Bobby were twin brothers. Billy said, "you always get to do things first," and Bobby said, "No, *you* always get to do things first." Who was right? Their parents said *neither* one was right. They tried to be fair and each boy got to be first one half of the time. But each of the boys saw the same thing from a different point of view and nothing seemed to change that simple fact.

Sometimes all you can do is recognize that you can see the same things from more than one point of view. It doesn't make one person right or wrong, they just don't agree. On the next page, you will see some optical illusions. Optical illusions are pictures that look different ways to different people, or even different ways to the same person! Can you see the two ways to look at each illusion?

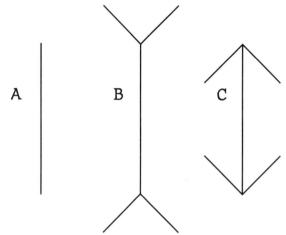

1. Which of these lines is the longest?

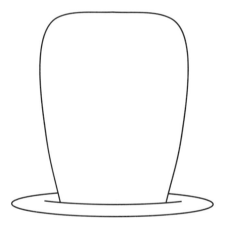

2. Is this hat higher than it is wide?

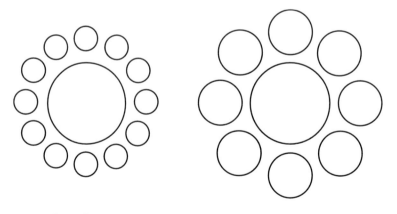

3. Which inner circle is the larger?

22. Your Family TV Show

Almost everyone watches TV shows about different families. You may notice that in every show someone in the family has a problem, and then it gets solved. Sometimes it gets solved in a funny way, sometimes in a more serious way.

Wouldn't it be fun to see your family on TV? To begin, make paper dolls of all the people in your family. You can paste on photographs or draw in each family member using the figures on the next page. Glue each figure to an index card and then cut them out. Then follow the directions to make a play TV out of an old box.

Now make up a TV show where something goes wrong in your family, and then you make it right!

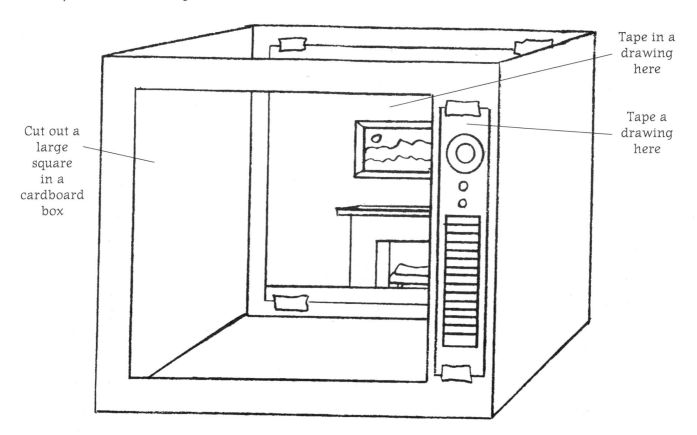

Tape in a drawing here

Tape a drawing here

Cut out a large square in a cardboard box

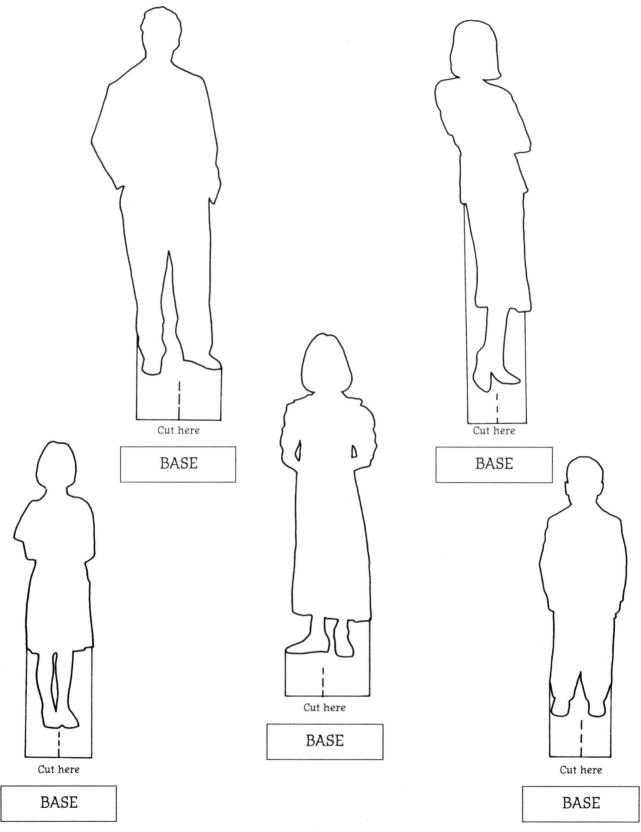

Cut here

BASE

Cut here

BASE

Cut here

BASE

Cut here

BASE

Cut here

BASE

64

23. A Garden Full of Friends

Imagine that you were planting a friendship garden. Everytime you did something nice for someone, it would be like planting a seed. Water it and a friend would pop up!

First you'll need the right seeds. Label the seed packets below to show what you need to "grow" your garden of friends.

24. A Future Full of Friends

Margie the Magician could see that her future was full of friends, because she knew the magic words to make friends appear! Can you fill in the missing letters below to learn her secret?

1. BE CO_SIDER_TE 2. S_ARE
3. _ELP OT_ERS 4. BE P_L_TE